LEXIS IN
WOLF'S CLOTHING

Poems by Mark Morgan Ford

Published by:
Cap & Bells Press
New York City, New York

www.capandbellspress.com

To my boys:
Liam Shea, Bryan Patrick, and Michael Colin

Acknowledgements

I would like to thank Timothy O'Sullivan and Jenny Lee Allen for their thoughtful readings and criticisms and especially Judith Strauss, my editor, for getting rid of so much that I should have never included and improving much of the rest.

Table of Contents

Lexis in Wolf's Clothing

In the dithyrambic early morning, thump, thump
I lollop toward you
(Or is it you to me?)
Hearts pumping, pulses racing!
Ecstatic, expectant, undaunted!
A grandee am I, a wizard, the Emperor's tailor,
boasting!
Scared shitless, I follow you,
Dressed in shimmering certainty,
With yards of silky thoughts to clothe my doubt

From the Orchard Keeper

Brindled midnight moonlight behind
Honeysuckle before him, climbing
Greening up the mountain's pebbled grayness

Too old for this, he struggled upwards
Stopping for breath on the rocky ledges
Wolves howling at the moon

Through a silhouette of branches
He saw it loping forward
Graceful movement in the dark

Through the narrow switchbacks
He followed, catching glimpses
Changeling in the speckled night

Finally, an opening to a lea and a pond
Where, head down, it was drinking
At ease, alone, or so it thought

Dropping to one leg he readied
Waiting for a signal
Like the beating of a heart

White road, scorched, snaking downward
He dragged it, heavy in his grip
Cherry orange was the rising sky

Bricolage: The Plan

A carpenter lies down by a river
Hope in his pockets
And a plan
A make-believe blueprint
For a make-believe boat
That can float on dust
On whatever lies between
Then and now
Based on an outline drafted
In invisible ink for constructing
Something, anything, that might
Carry him forward
Made from bits and pieces
Of his life, remembered
Or invented, that are
Now hidden in
His pockets

For me
For a good reason
Whatever it was that made the river
That glistening, pixilated surface
With that lilac dark current flowing
Noiselessly underneath
Had, after so many years, gone
And the river was dry as dust

That was fine with me
But then one morning
Digging into my pockets I found:

A pair of cufflinks that weren't mine
(Platinum with an ebony center)
A folded handkerchief, monogrammed
(Whose initials I didn't know)
Three counterfeit bills in a silver clip
And an unfamiliar pink plastic cellphone
That, though cracked, still held a charge

What do you do with stuff like that
That appears, unremembered?

Here's what I decided:
I'd wrap the cufflinks in the handkerchief
Clip the money to the cellphone
See how that looked, and if I didn't like it
I'd put the money in the handkerchief
And wrap the cufflinks in the money, etc.
And if, while doing so,
That phone should ring
I'd answer it

CB 1: Renewal

Damn, so this is how it happens:
After a year or ten or forty
Struggling to do something
That could fetch with time
A good idea of yourself
You wake up one morning
And in the shrill fluorescent light
See too clearly the fault lines
Or, coming down to breakfast,
The banality of it all
Not just of your vanities
But of every thing you know
Then later, after work,
Less disappointing than usual,
You go out on the fire escape
For a drink and a smoke
And looking out at the city,
You feel, once again,
The faintest building buzz
Maybe it's the booze or
Maybe it's a memory
There's always a memory
Perhaps of that book
Written by what's his name
That person you didn't trust
That surprised you and then,
Fuck yes, delighted you
The images were crisp
But even better – visible
And that made the sentiments

Believable and that always
Amazes you…
And even better
Were the little stories
That reminded you that
We all have stories
Even you –
And you notice you have not lit
The little Italian Toscanello
Imported implausibly through
Scranton, Pennsylvania
And even that inspires you
Somehow to think that…
Hell yes, you can do this

CB 2: The Happy Tank

I have tried smiling in the mirror
Telling myself *ad nauseum*
Attitude is everything
And it is – I don't dispute it
But this morning
Putting my sore feet
Down beside my bed
I felt something
I could not deny
It was the piercing
Prick of the regular –
I hate to use the word
But it works – ennui
It is a painful poke
From the universe
A crude postcard
From the surrounding void
Its message bluntly written
In permanent ink:
You are empty

Yes, here I am again with
Nothing in the happy tank

See here – where I'm touching?
It is a hollow thing
A container where once
Spontaneously ambition
From who knows where
Arrived every day

And so I sit here waiting
Waiting for that to happen
Wondering how the tank emptied
Thinking that I might have slept poorly
Or suffered bad dreams or woken too soon
But none of that feels like an explanation
And so I'm left with the anxious thought
That tomorrow and the next day
It will be the same

CB 3: Simile

Like a tree uprooted
Or limbless, leafless –
Damn! Which is it?
> Like a firecracker without a fuse
> A fishing pole without a line
> A bicycle wheel without spokes
> A wooden chair without one leg…
I can't get it right
In the old days there was so much –
Almost too much
> A cur licking its crotch in a patch of sun
> A scraggy thatch palm in a cypress grove
> A woman in black in the
> Shadow of a doorway
> On Via Condotti, in Rome
> (Waiting, I was sure, for me)
Buoyant in the rising tide of ignorance
I feel sometimes like a nova
Still white-hot but cooling fast
Soon I'll be left with nothing but
Some small length of time or space
So I must start with this:
> This firecracker
> This fishing line
> This bicycle wheel
> This wooden chair

CB 4: To Say Goodbye

If I could say goodbye
Could wrap this life (or any other)
In white linen and lay it down
Gently on a wooden float and
Nudge it, gently, out onto
A runaway river –

Or dress it in chemicals
And a suit of charcoal gray
Place it neatly in a tufted box
Dig a grave, lower it in,
And, throwing dirt on it,
Abandon it forever, I would

If I could build a pyre
Or any sort of sacred fire
And use it to burn up
The flesh and bone of grief
I would, I would

I would but I can't or I won't
And so I don't
Which is why you are here
With me now, still
After all these years
All of you

I don't want to make a list
For it will make you less
Than what you are… still

I *am* willing to let you go
More than willing, I'm eager
But it must be in small degrees
One gesture or word at a time

Everything I Wanted to Know

Once, stoned, I looked at my hand
And it wasn't a hand anymore
But an outcropping of land in the sea
And I recognized that the sea was
Larger, infinitely larger, than I was
And that I could no longer separate
The stable land from the roiling sea
And what was once a hand was now
And would probably always be
A molecular universe
Of pulsing, incomprehensible noise
And that if I could read it I could know it
But I would never know it
Because the I that I was was no longer
And the vast sea of atomic dust was
In me and outside of me and was me

Once, under laughing gas, I saw
That the secret of the universe was
Not hidden away as I had thought
But was on sale nearly everywhere
And was available in every language
And the secret was this:
That life was a joke in the
Never-ending posture of
Laughing at itself
And if you think about it
You can see that a hand in space
Is that sort of joke

The Poet's Necklace

Hoping to fabricate a string of pearls
He makes instead a fragile necklace
Of thoughts soft as baby onions
Strung together with a thread of hope
Thinner than his veins and forming
A loop that fits, just roughly, the shape
Of his ambition and yet cannot be worn,
He fears, beyond the limits of his life

And Now This Time Is Welcome

These days I am slower in movement
But quicker to say, "No more of this."

This one's fragile superiority
A sun-bleached sparrow's bone, snaps

From a single sharp yank of truth
And in breaking restores a friendship

That one's neediness, enfolded
In billowy sentiments, collapses

Under the weight of half the gravity
Honest judgment brings to bear

And somehow, against all odds
Lets something good get free

And my own porcelain narcissism
Hard to the touch as polished steel

Shatters inexplicably one morning
While shaving and reveals in fluorescent light

A surprising, amorphous face

Positano

Along the shore of the *Spiaggia Grande*
The slender fishing boats are anchored closely
Like fountain pens on a desktop of crumpled green
paper
Beside the shore, barefoot boys play a game of soccer
The edges of their shouts and laughter rising
Happily above the grumbling surf

I'm sitting here next to you on our balcony
On the other balcony, the sisters have come out
The pair of them – old and gnarled – to watch the
sun set
One bent and twisted over the balustrade like a
grapevine
The other, in her wheelchair, face frozen, looking up

It's late in the afternoon and I want to believe
Every sight and sound counts for something
A truck starting its engine, shutters closing
A door opening, a dog barking in the valley

I'm not talking because I'm listening and
I'm listening because I'm trying to remember
Because I am so bad at remembering
And I know there's a chance this will be it
You know – my last trip to Positano with you

When He Kissed Me

Something
Was there, even now, is there
Ecstatic, electrifying – an energetic field
Of atomic space, surrounding us, luminescent

When he bent down to kiss me it snowed
And some kind of icy feeling sluiced down my chest
Prompted goosebumps on the skin that was both
our skins
And cut a cold stream to the ocean of what we knew

Ataraxia

I can't relax
Though I try
I want to go soft
Liquid soft, yielding
Move like mercury
Yet I feel heavy
And that's not good

I want to defy gravity
Rise above myself
Lifted by my own breath
I am getting denser
I don't like it

I want to thin out, be
As thin as aluminum foil
And then thinner still
But I am nothing like that
I am a black hole
And everything around me,
Including you,
Is adding to my weight

I want to shed light
Not attract it
Lightness will come eventually
It always does – and often just in time
But I want to get there on my own

Planes and Surfaces

A compass needle angled at thirty degrees
Against the flat surface of drafting paper
A Queen Palm, upright against the horizon
A vertical stroke against a horizontal blue line

A seated body
Bent over a laptop
Is an "a"
A standing body
Looking out the window
Is an italicized "I"
A loved one
Cast away
Is an "r"
A loved one
Invited back
Is a "y"

There is horizontality to everything
That makes elevation difficult to bear
You do your best, you put on, for example,
Mozart's Adagio in G Minor
Open the door and let in some brightness
You go on, doing your best
Because you know
That eventually
Because of some law of physics
As yet unnamed
But not unnoticed
Everything will flatten out

Falling Things

It's tough to make something useful out of falling
things
You can do something with the rain or snow or the
sunset
But that's not – I know you'll agree – the same
However good you are at metaphor
You won't be able to write something helpful
Or adamantine or both or either
Out of something falling
And there will be
Always
Something falling
Shadows
Dust
Embers
Bodies
Leaves…
Disconnected from branches
That are now too old or brittle to be of any good
Like the answers you get from lovers
You failed to love or loved too well

Last Night When You Outed Me

Last night, in front of friends, you announced
Half kiddingly, perhaps to take the edge off,
That I was a misogynist – and people sort of laughed
Yet you were right and we all knew it

My life of loving women is divided, like Gaul,
Into three parts, my mother, my first lover, and you
My mother had eight children
She did the best she could
Imagine a pie cut into eight pieces
It is not an infinitely expanding thing
So I don't blame her
I got what was mine
My first lover loved me like a child
That finds a toy on Christmas
Unwraps greedily the wrapping
Holds it up to the light
Is delighted and then moves on
That is as much as we can expect
But still, it is not enough and that
That is the person you had at the start

I'd like to remind you of so many things
Do you remember, for example, when, back then…
How we walked on 16th Street on Sundays,
When the air was crisp and everything was green
And I liked saying I was "so happy to be alive"?
It was a cliché but you knew I meant it
And you knew I meant to say how much
I meant to do to keep us happy and safe

But you never said what you were thinking
Perhaps because you feared it was
Already, for both of us, too late

You Are Here

Everything spreads out
Jade and glittering
Along the horizon
Or so it seems when we are young
And our lens is wide open
Yet now, from here, just above
The surface of the deck and pool
Under the pavilion's clay-tiled roof
Sheltered from the sun's white heat
The garden, breathing, beckons
Luminous and green, inviting
And almost makes us believe
We can enter paradise
By the mere act of knocking
At the doors of eternity

In the Basement of OK Cigars

Have you ever made your own envelopes? It's a
hobby of mine.
It's just a thing, kind of strange...
I thought of doing that, but I was afraid the postman
might object.
Like not sending it, or holding it up for some stupid
technical reason.
Is there a legal standard for envelopes?
I don't know man. I don't even know if there *should* be.

I'm really skeptical of stamps these days – that they
will stay on.
Like especially ever since they came up with self-
sticking stamps.
For sure. You see the edges curling up and you
wonder...
They might not make it through the scanners!
That wouldn't be cool.
I think about putting tape on it but I wonder if the
dudes at the post office would have a problem with
that. I just want it to go to where it's going.

My dad has a massive stamp collection. As a kid I
had to soak envelopes to get them off. That's all I did
for years. The sink would get clogged up with glue.
The slugs would eat the stuff.
I had to pick dandelions in the yard with one of
those two-pronged pickers because my parents were
hippies and wouldn't use weed spray.
But it's work, man, and work is good.

It's better than doing dishes, I guess.

I can't watch people doing dishes. It drives me crazy when they don't rinse them right.
Yeah, it's bad, it's really bad.
I am so obsessed with rinsing.
Me too. Do you use the rack or dry them with a towel?
I use the rack, man. Why would I go to all that trouble of rinsing them and then wipe them with a crappy towel?

It's like having a washcloth in the shower.
I haven't seen one of those in ages.
So old school.
It's not right, man. It's just not right.

Tina C's Dreams

In her dream I am a large white tiger
Moving stealthily through the grass
She runs but cannot run fast enough
She is fresh meat and I am hungry
I am Balthus, the painter, and she is
A child draped over a velvet chair
She poses a hundred ways for me
Eating cookies, drinking chocolate milk
I am never satisfied with the light
She was born to be a lucky dragon but now
She is my fragile, bird-boned quarry
Running breathless through the forest
Believing she is something other than
What I see – my mouth-watering prey
One day she will tire of running
And lay her body down on the grass
And, looking up at me, eyes wet,
See her own inevitable end

Fifth of July

The koi fish are fat now, that's good
But I am fat too – back to my old fat self
I am envious of the un-self-reflective,
Un-ambiguous, un-relenting, un-consciousness of fish

Last night the fireworks were encouraging
Explosions of color against a backdrop of gloom
But I cannot stop thinking
About the undeniable fact that I am fat
Yes, there are these flashes, these great colors
But when the smoke clears it is black

Everything But

Banish my pistachio ice cream
Confiscate my Nicaraguan cigars
Hide my Razor golf clubs and Mont Blanc pens
Give my NSX to the junkman, toss my iPhone in the
trash
You can even shutter up the windows
And drape the paintings on the walls
But don't – please don't – bright out my dark moods
For sometimes I need to feel my own collapsing

To A

In Greece you spent a month in the mountains
Reading the old poets, growing a beard
Coming down Sunday mornings to the village
To buy bread and cheese or sausage
But with your rough-hewn look and
Speaking, as you did, in the old tongue
The merchants stared at you, aghast,
Believing you some mountain ghost

Years later, at Yale, you told me that your goal
Was to be lauded by critics, a blurb on your books
proclaiming:
"He changed the modern view of Plato
And Homer and the other ancient poets
While simultaneously inflaming
Beyond acceptable tolerances
The passions of a thousand coeds"

In our high school days I think you might have
Just might have needed me – was that the case?
I hope not for I was mean and unforgiving
And yet you somehow found your way
And later even a way to forgive me

These days we see each other once a year
At family gatherings where you give
When the moment calls, the most articulate toasts
And dance madly like some Dionysian spirit
And sing like Sappho in harmony with your siblings
And laugh like Saturn and reminisce with us
Arguing happily late into the night

The Americans

It's Hoboken on the Fourth of July
A parade is marching down the street
Above, from a pair of casement windows
Whose frames, in despair, have buckled,
Two women in weary housecoats
Plump sausage-arms, leaning, looking out
The building's façade is indolent, uncaring
Between them a great, billowing American flag

Prelude in G Major

Here is how I imagine you:
Sunk deep in an old leather chair in an English Library
Reading an old book of some still obscure importance
The room has a smoky odor, the carpet is worn but
rich
Sun comes in through a skylight illuminating your
shoulder

Or you are at the reins of a horse-drawn carriage
Racing through countryside toward the city
Where the Prime Minister will praise you
(Then later, in darkness, you will fondle his daughter)

In my mind, this makes your genius deeper
And your scope that much wider
Which, astute readers will surmise,
Says more about me than about you

I Haven't Been Completely Honest

This is what I haven't told you: You are *not* my buddy
Comrade, pal, compatriot, chum, or main man
I resent your smug certainty that you know me
Your condescending questions, your supercilious
laugh
And your habit of coming into my house uninvited
Traipsing through it, leaving your footprints
And yet in some way I do love you
And that is something I have to think about

Mutatis Mutandis

I have filed away my best work
Burned what I cannot finish
Written short letters to old friends

I've boxed up all my books
Wrapped up in brown paper
The packages I've meant to send

I've soaked my feet in warm water
And carried the water jug, now empty
Back to the well again

Now all that remains is to wait
With you for night's arrival

Dinny Cronin, RIP, 2011

Dinny Cronin, beloved family friend
Lifetime lover of one-eyed Tiffany-girl Mary Jane
Sire to a scraggly brood of Irish wunderkinds
Jane and John and Joseph and Jenny, et al.
Our ersatz cousins in wit and whiskey
Yet dissimilar in some undeclared way
That would separate us as time trudged on

You worked in a city (that is a different city now)
Of defunct unions and affable criminals
One polished black boot in Damon Runyon
And the other in Basketball Diaries
I see you walking down Bowery Street
In the early morning, steam rising from the subway
vents
Wet newspapers, unreadable, on the sodden street
Hands in your pockets, telling beggars to fuck off

Once, when I was left in the lurch, you called me
onto the porch
And dressed me down but offered to "take care of
the situation"
For which I am still shocked and scared and grateful

What Thota Lost

In Warangal, the paper said,
One Thota sold for thirty lakh
Two acres of good land
And hid it in a plastic drum
Beneath other drums and whatnot
And went to sleep untroubled
Dreaming of his bride to be
A short circuit ignited the fire
That blazed eagerly through his house
Seventy quitals of cotton were lost
Two domestic LPG cylinders
And seven plastic drums
Fire control trucks from Parkai
Responded to the alarm
But were delayed by fate
Arriving just as Thota understood
The full count of what was lost

Come and Get Me

Howl if you want
Beat your chest!
Lunge forward!
Trample me!

I am waiting

Neck deep in mud
Alert but immobile
I see your eyes burning
To consume me

I am waiting

Your powerful hands
Clutch my throat
To throttle me

I am not yet done
But waiting

Walt Whitman

On Pennsylvania Avenue on Inauguration Day
Walt Whitman saw Abe Lincoln, riding
On horseback to and from the Capitol
In Lincoln's face Whitman saw compassion
And a "hearty tenderness" that he took as manly
But also indelible lines of something worse than worry
That time and the vast and terrible struggle had etched

Earlier, near the front, he walked among the wounded
Giving out bandages purchased on a clerk's pay
And saw in the faces of the injured boys
Pride and fear and grief and loss and sorrow
There were, he knew, no hearts undamaged
And those marks would be on the unborn
A legacy of self-doubt masked by temerity
Or unexamined charity or universal benevolence

How to Start Over Again

The following technique is effective
When used in a controlled environment:
(A thousand repetitions are required for mastery,
Therefore you should begin immediately)

Imagine that her eyes are sparkling green
Picture her lips: pink, pouty, parted
See the upturned nose, how her fine hair
Falls loosely over her sunburned shoulders

                                   Or…

(And this has been proven to work for some
With a single repetition): Return to your childhood
Rape your mother, kill your father,
Leave the knife, let the back door slam behind you

When Everything Mattered

Then I was so full of care
Aware of every pulse and shade
I could barely step into a room
Or hear a passing, thoughtless statement
Without worry or watchfulness or wonder

In that endlessly blooming world
Every word was a budding seed
Every gesture a shift of wind
Shadows might signal rain or relief
Light had a hundred puzzling colors

Now I don't listen for I've heard it before
Nor look – for what is there I haven't seen?

Yet now and then I remember bits and pieces –
A churchgoer fumbling to open his wallet
A teacher stumbling over a familiar phrase
Your younger self foretelling our future

Last night, for example, almost dreaming,
I felt crazy scared about losing you
Then sleep, as it always does, came
And morning woke me careless

Propinquity

The door cracked and there he was,
Wild eyes blazing, the familiar brows
His smile as crooked as a country road
Past Ballyshannon and Bundoran
And up to Donegal and then to Bogh
On which some distant cousin could
Return and find his way back home

"It's me," I said, "your long-lost kin."
He looked me up and down
"And if you are, so what?"
So what indeed, so what?
And then he stepped away and let me in

Discipline

This morning, after we argued
I could not eat
But as the afternoon passed I got hungry
And ached for macaroni and cheese

Tonight, perhaps at dinner, we'll talk again
And I will, after dinner, admit I was wrong
Which will make you feel satisfied
And make me hungry again

Controlling the appetite, Gandhi said,
Is helpful in controlling the mind
Who could argue with that?

BPF

When I returned from the hospital
You were watching a soccer match
And I thought, "In the middle of the day?"
I asked you something about the game –
Who was winning or playing or such –
And we had that bit of a conversation
Then you asked what I was doing
I have a shitload of writing to do,
I said, and I'm eager to get back to it,
But I spent the morning in the hospital
With David B, you remember David B,
Don't you – my old Peace Corps friend?
Well, after conquering the world, he is dying
And that, as it might have, ended the conversation
Later, on the porch, writing and thinking
That we'd missed the mark by so small a margin,
Through the opened den window
On the other side of the house,
Music – some strange and troubled music –
You were playing, or not playing but composing,
Good and worthy work for your separate world

LSFF

You surprised me
Again
The brave idea
Renouncing
The sure
For the improbable
There you are
In a steeplechase
Riding tall and
Jumping
Over barricades
Or there in an armory
Masked, fencing
Scoring
Being scored upon
And there
On a country road
Running, stopping
Shooting
And there
At the edge of a pool
Crouched, alert
Then swimming
No, racing
For your life

Cognitive Psychology

Complexity sometimes requires
The simplicity of simple illusions
Such as when, if, after drinking too much,
You fall off your chair and vomit a bit
In front of forty startled diners, you can,
If you don't overthink it, get back up again
And announce with a sort of dignity
That your medication "didn't agree" with you

D's Tattoos

He spends the morning grousing at nurses
And the afternoon dozing off in front of the TV
I stand at the foot of his bed and look at him
His body, once strong, is thin now – even frail
Around his biceps tattoos I've never seen before
Faded black symbols that once
Must have meant something
Some statement about who he was or
Wanted to be, some testimony to his
Bold and dramatic youth – which I knew
Only from his letters and later from stories
He told me whenever we could be alone
I believed them all as well as I could
But I can't believe them now
Here in this anonymous room
Watching his chest rise and fall
Each breath a bit weaker than before

One Step and You Are There

You are on the threshold
It's now or never, you believe
If you get away now the world
And all its many surprises
Will be unwrapped for you
You will grow a scruffy beard
Wear a wide-brimmed hat
And sunglasses – yes, sunglasses
Travel to Granada, rent a room
A shuttered room with a single
Incandescent light bulb and chain
In the back of the old *Hotel Colonial*
You will write mornings like Papa
Walk to the *Parque Central* at noon
Where Nestor holds your table
In the far corner, overlooking the square
There you will eat *el carne del día*
Read *El Diario*, sip a *café Americano*
And shoo away children selling trinkets
And you will be a handsome stranger
And your Spanish will be perfect
And your work will all be good
And the evening will come slowly

Don't Kid Yourself

You pretend to be a Jacobin
Bright. Red. Righteous.
But you are nothing of the kind
Nor a lord, nor his knight
But if anything
A jester
In a court of fools
Not a raconteur
But a kibitzer
Jabbering
To a clutch of cranes
Not a gifted writer
But a factotum
Intemperate, needy
Begging for his master's love

Reading the Morning Papers

In the morning, over coffee
I take an inventory of the assets
My heart – a sturdy machine
My mind – a sharpened razor
My hands – rugged and supple
Check, check, check

Yet reading the morning paper I discover
That the sky is not the blue canopy
I once again expected but a sooty roof
And though you are speaking to me
I can't hear you because all the strength
Of my attention has gone out of me
And puddled into this inky gospel of doom

These Will Inherit My Earth

All these I include in my kingdom:

The brave that step out into the storm
Heads high against the pelting rain
Forgiving their parents' failures
Remembering ancestral journeys

The strong that do not suffer fools
Though fools are their culture's darlings
Disrobing the popular myths
Revealing what is false or foul

The honest that bear witness
To the simple hidden truths
Rebuking the pedestrian gossip
Making common cowards prickle

These are the chosen few, my heirs
Sparkling in the darkness of our time

Le Mot Juste

I've been thinking
The poet says
About how
Complicit he is in
So many things
      And then waits
Listening for a heartbeat
He has never stopped
Hoping for despite
Every bit of evidence
Life has given him
That he's a fool
      Because he believes
Against all evidence that there is
      Out there, somewhere
His perfect soul mate
Waiting for him to utter
Just the correct words
      He's tried so many things
A bundled cuteness
A specious profundity
An extreme sensitivity
      And now this –
A declaration of complicity
The hope that a crafted thought
Could both implicate and
Absolve him from his
Original sin – a selfish
And foolish vanity

What It Takes

A morning's unfiltered sunlight
A plate of eggs and toast
An idea or ambition from
A walk along the coast

An afternoon's quiet shade
A table in the cloister
A page as white as snowfall
A plot or poem to braid

An evening's welcomed darkness
A drink, a notebook, a cigar
A heart of foolish courage
The distant, waking stars

Dressing for the Future

My shirt, wet, is a window looking on to
The landscape of my collapsing hopes

My pants pockets, bulging, are wheelbarrows
Heavy with the litter of a million mistakes

My knee socks, pulled tight,
Hide the swollen veins of naïve ambition

Only my shoes, tiny trucks of the future,
Have a patina of hope for marching on

Love as a Puzzle

The missing pieces are the shapes that complete us
Silhouettes that form a portrait in reverse
We want what is natural, our wholeness, but lack
Even an outline of what we wish to be

Don't Let the Others Know

Don't let the others know…
But today is the promised flood
Whose rising surface will lift
The vessels of hopefulness and delight

Yesterday was a passing nothingness
In a dead sea of extinguished wants
That suggest in their absence
Every promise time makes up

All that and more will be tomorrow
But tomorrow is already disappearing
Into what was a future that is lost

Looking Out

An aura illuminates a familiar Maine landscape
The boy, nose to the cool glass, looks out
Hoping to see in the gloaming a fawn
That passed, ghost-like, the previous night

In Key West a man sits at the bar of the Blue Heaven
Smoking and watching the diners come and leave
Imagining that he too could become a prizefighter
Or a writer or a fisherman if he had more time

On Long Island a woman lies in a sunroom
Looking out at an old Jacaranda tree
Whose purple flowers bloom so briefly
She wonders if she might have missed them

I Should Get Rid of You

There have been moments
Okay, thousands of them,
When I have thought that
I should bury you
Put you into moist soil
And let the flesh, bone, blood, etc.
That cannot have been you
Decompose as the years go by
Waiting for something new
To replace you on the good chance that
Anything will be an improvement
Because, let's be honest, we all know
You are the faulty byproduct of an imperfect plan
That shows in nearly everything you do
A kind of artifice – your posture, your gait
The way you cannot really smile, and in
Your wit, your wisdom, and the way
You look back at me in the morning
When I'm brushing my teeth

For JS: The Final Edit

He drags it in like a trophy
Leaving a trickle of blood on the floor
Happy to be hunting at his age
Proud to leave it for you at the door

Its feet are skeletal, imponderable
Its wings curl inwards, in disrepair
Its eyes are closed, its legs folded
A mess of splintered bones and bloody feathers

You have, he knows, shears to trim the ragged edges
A set of braces for the crooked legs
Two beads of colored glass to serve as eyeballs
And your heart so its heart can beat again

When the Gods Came

The pilgrims were on their way
Tickets bought, rooms reserved
Planes and buses boarded
Eager to witness the great event

The announcement was shocking
Coming, as it did, from the president
Who had succeeded to office
On an all-atheist platform

But the next day it was confirmed
First by the pope in Rome
Next by a rabbi in Jerusalem
And finally by Tibetan monks

All through the day they assembled
Wearing *The Gods Are Coming!* tee shirts and
sipping Coke
Vendors in sombreros sold hot dogs and falafel
The mood, everyone agreed, was electric

Then, at sunset, the skyline,
A great violet curtain, opened
And the gods flew in – all the great gods
And a thousand lesser deities

"For so many years we have been with you
And have served you well," they sang,
"Bathed you in hope, anointed you in faith
And delivered you safely from evil.

"But now we are old and weary
Done with answering your stupid pleas.
It's time for us to lie down and rest.
From now on, you're on your own."

And then, one by godly one, they lay down
On the shore and disappeared into the sand
And the crowds stood there waiting and waiting
For the next big thing

For Fanny

Fanny, you are ill
The un-apprehended thought
That is always in the space between us
Has settled in the marrow of your fragile bones
And will soon be thick in our hearts

Laughter

Dogs laugh – did you know that?
That happy panting – that's laughter.
Record it and then play it back.
Mad or anxious dogs will settle down.

Apes laugh and monkeys do too.
Humans? We laugh most of all.
Laughter, they've discovered, is contagious.
In fact, it's the most contagious thing we do.

Eskimos laugh more than any other people.
They laugh even in the blistering cold.
Once a man in England started laughing
On a TV show and kept laughing for an hour.

In Africa there have been plagues of laughter –
Entire villages laughing for weeks at a time.
Specialists were flown in to put a stop to it,
But they ended up laughing too.

Coming home last evening
I passed a school playground
Full of laughing children.

I wanted to stop and watch them,
Understand that kind of laughter,
But I was late and we had problems.
I had to get back and study you.

Another Possible Sign

The Web – which is to say the world – was on it
A boy, a freckle-faced eight-year-old, was gone
All the righteous people were righteously outraged
It was one great outpouring of fear and fun and
        desperation
Of saccharine sentiments and self-congratulations
        and tripe
While back in the underworld, the brick-and-
        mortar universe
Of that second, parallel universe, in the shattered
        rooms of the forgotten,
Rivulets of blood, red and glittering, ran
Each drop a universe of living cells
Flowing from a constellation of undiscovered
        human hearts
Running over the linoleum and under the doors
And down the porch steps and onto the sidewalk
And there to the city streets and on and on and
        finally into the river
Where the water turned into a fluent of foaming red
Leaving those that still fished dumbstruck
And through it all you slept soundly beside me
As if the moon and the stars and the sun
Were waiting there with us, waiting for
The blood to dry up and everything to begin again

After We Drank Too Much

It was Lou and his new girl, Samantha, and I
At the bar on a still-hot October midnight
After the boxing match, after we drank too much
Dead air, a month before the end of hurricane season
Talking happily about the old days, when men were
men, etc.
It was fine, it really was, but then Lou took it
                              – a beat too far

And suddenly the sky parted and the rain came down
And she left us there
Lou standing there, slack-jawed
"That fucking bitch! She has the car!"
I sat down on the pavement in front of the place
Lou just stood there looking down that empty road
Weary, I lay back, my hands behind my head, and dozed
Some time later I woke and Lou was standing above me

Goddamn it, girl, this is bullshit
You can't run off like that, taking my ride
Leaving us here, no fucking way, man
Get back here and take us home!

He was pacing back and forth above and behind me
It made me dizzy
I thought of that painting
The Scream, and closed my eyes
                              – and then

I was standing on that bridge, trembling
And the bridge was wobbly in the current
And the stream, in that dream, had a name
And the name was Anger and it flowed
Flowing into the wider, deeper river
Called The River of Regret that ran and ran
And emptied into the sea and the sea was called
The Sea of Extinction and it said so on the map
And the map itself was called The Map of Life
                                        – and then

Lou was still pacing, but beside me and slower

Come on, girl, this ain't right
You can't treat me like this, goddamn it
Or just think about my friend
You better come get us, baby, now!

My head was a dense, heavy, sodden brick
I opened my eyes
                                        – and there, above me

Tree branches clutching, parking meters melting
The sky, starry, spinning but still I reached out
Reaching for that phone, but Lou didn't notice
And so I lay back down and closed my eyes

I was the director and star of a black and white movie
A moonlit field of tall grass in an unfamiliar land
Around me, in the distance, shrouded figures moved
And the eerie, plaintive sound of something crying
But I was safe, encased in a shield of light
                                        – and then

Come on baby,
Please, don't leave me
I love you babe, you know that
Come on back!

I sat up, feeling better, good enough to smile
"Give me that thing," I said, "I'll show you how it's done."
And then I called you and you asked the time
It was nearly dawn
But you sat up and looked out the window to our sea
And asked for my whereabouts and called a taxi

Ancient Creatures

In the black cool of the sea bottom
Soft-bodied creatures dwell
Blind and mute, moving slowly
As they have for a million years
With these ancient ancestors
We share some bits of DNA
So it's not crazy to imagine
When life is too harsh and strident
How good it would be to dwell
Unobserved and thoughtless
Gliding through the beautiful dark

At the End of Her Illness

After a protracted suffering she lies
Still as stone, her body an effigy
Her mind, a tethered crow,
Her eyes reflecting the roiling night

Her once fine and beautiful hands
Are folded in her lap, broken twigs
Her feet, like ivory talons, arch
The body is a shell, barely breathing

Yet through her eyes
I see that she wants
To tell me something
I don't want to know

And my heart is beating
Pumping out questions
That should have been
Answered years ago

An Almanac of Me and You

We've been together all 200 seasons
Crisp autumns watching the leaves fall
Cold winters when walking we snapped
Frail, frozen branches underfoot
Spring's gathering hopefulness and
Summer's long stretches of lackluster heat

We've had a heap of loud discussions
Spoken earnestly when we had to
Lied as carefully as care would
Stood so long from one another at
A close distance and then
Came together when we could

The Keys

On the way home I lost something
I'm trying to figure out what it was
Passing over the threshold I could feel it was missing
And that saddened me though I didn't know why
It's hard to keep much of anything these days
In my bag or in my pockets or in my head
I can do an inventory of what I should carry
A wallet with cards, cash, a phone, keys
Maybe that is what was missing, the keys
Not the car keys, of course, or the house keys
But that ring of keys that once could unlock
The doors that opened
Or might still open
Into the rooms of your heart

Late Mourning

She had me stand next to her
In front of the open grave
As if to signal to the assembled
That there was continuity
He and I then he and she then she and I
      Or maybe to comfort me, I couldn't tell
I stood there, unwilling to make a scene
Her small hand looped around my forearm
It was cold and wet, we were shivering
I could not or didn't want to hear the eulogy
Those always disappointing words
I was wondering how – really – he had died
The official story, simple bad luck,
Was preposterous
But some stories are built as bridges
That span currents we can't bear to cross
If it was for his mother, then okay, I understood
But still I was curious – or more than that bothered
I never found out, but now I can see it didn't matter
I was already, then, beyond grief, past mourning
I'd buried him several years earlier
When it was just he and his gang of losers
Drug addicts and sycophants and moochers
That infested his hideaway apartment near the bar
I was back in town on business and I went by
And when he answered the door, it was in his eyes
He barely recognized me, but invited me in
I followed him into the living room and we sat for a
while
Amidst his deadbeat entourage, nodding
Hammered by the music, the relentless music

That I remember still
And there was nothing done and nothing said
I told him I had a plane to catch and he shrugged
So I embraced his unresponsive body and put my face
Against his cold ear and whispered then
That I missed and would always remember him
That was my eulogy, to him, half conscious but alive

Italy Again

Italy is once again bankrupt
Bankers are suited whores
Governors are their pimps
The lawyers shit on the law
Doctors do not heal
Teachers do not teach
Workers go on strike
"Nobody wants to work anymore,
Not even the artists and drag queens,
And why should they?"
Italy is bankrupt
And yet in Tuscany along the hilltops
Cypress trees still stand tall
Beside the ancient ochre villas
Jade sentinels guarding something
In Rome a cobbled alley opens
Into an ancient piazza where women
In shawls sell fruit and flowers
And in Venice the gondolas glide between
The afternoon's folded shadows
Reminding us that this country
Is not a country but a place we want to be

Elephant Caves

In Mumbai, after the lunatic streets near the harbor,
the fuming buses, battered
Cars, rickety bicycles and tuk-tuks inserting
themselves in the momentary spaces…

The boys in designer jeans on mopeds with their
girlfriends in saris behind them
And always, impossibly, the stray dog lying
unperturbed in everything's way…

We boarded the ferry that groaned as it rocked in
the water, carrying farmers,
Schoolchildren and their teachers, and sailors
through the smoke and salty air

Then on Elephant Island, we stood inside a temple,
cut so impossibly by hand
From a mountainside of granite to form a temple the
size of an airplane hangar

To be there, finally, amid the ancient gods – one for
creation, one for protection,
One for destruction, one for rebirth – in that unreal
hardscape of shadows

To contemplate our many incarnations, each
separate but connected by this thin
Tissue of memory and/or imagination – I'm too old
to know which it is

To count up everything we have produced and
measure it against how much
We thought it might have been and how little it
seems now, next to this

The House That Words Built

I never gave you the house I promised
So I will build it for you now
On this lot of palms and sea grass
In front of the softly rolling sea
I'll build it from old pine and limestone
With cypress ceilings and teakwood beams
Black shutters, white window casements
Stucco walls painted lemon and
A roof of terra cotta tiles
I'll make a big kitchen with marble counters
And a dining room big enough for sixteen
Beside that we'll have a salon and a piano room
And a library where I can stack my books
Our bedroom will have a balcony with a view
And there will be three guest rooms
One for each of our children
And a garden cottage for a friend
And in every room there will be art
And chairs, extra chairs, for anyone
Who wants to stop by and sit
And marvel at what we've done

Malicious Children

It was said she was rich once, before
Something terrible happened
Now a madwoman in a shredded dress
Pushing a junk-filled shopping cart
We teased her and she ran after us
A freight car uncoupled from its engine
Like pigeons we scattered before her
Our hearts mad with malicious delight

Aren't We Something!

Hell, yes! Let's agree that we are special
The apotheosis of some intelligent design
Finely crafted machines with gilded cogs
Turning in synchronicity and not, for sure,
Some viscous inchoate liquid, spreading
Over every natural thing: the green fields
Of time and the white oceans of space

Stuff That Happens

I walked into a bar late at night
An old man was there, no one else
He said, What do you want, pussy?
I ordered a drink… The bar's closed, he said

I got a letter from Celestine, a writer's wife,
She said her husband was a pervert, not a writer
I sent her the book we wrote together
She told me to keep my fucking hands to myself

I was tied up and thrown into a ditch
The kid that did it to me was sort of cool
I've often wondered if he loved me
Lots of people hurt people they love

The Choreographer

She has the day planned
Four Buddhist temples
Three good meals
Two exhausting treks
One blissful night

She is very good at this
A choreographer of fun
But sometimes the dance
Is too much for a dancer
Whose knees are old
Who'd rather sit still
At the bank of a river
Watching boats pass

Yet when he dreams
He is fleet and agile
And in the morning
He realizes that the dance
Gives him another chance

The Brilliant Love Affair

Whatever it was flagged out in June
By August she was in Massachusetts
He stayed in the attic in the heat
Masturbating and planning his future

In the autumn she came back at midnight
Sneaking into the house, slipping into his bed
She was on her way to Puerto Rico, she said
He could go with her if he wanted

That winter he worked two shifts for money
And to make his body strong and his mind cold
In dreams she came back to him, broken
Singing a song he'd written long before

The Extinction Event

Here, in this bed, everything is nearly perfect
Warm light is coming through the shutters
Landing on the crumpled sheets where you lay
I've been up already for hours

You woke when I did and thought to get baguettes
And got out of bed and dressed and got on the bike
And then, at the corner, you turned and went down
And that great alive thing that was your consciousness
Was suddenly gone – just like that

But I don't know that yet and so I'm still lying here
Feeling the morning sun
In a few minutes, I'll go downstairs
And to keep busy while I wait,
Make some coffee and set the table

RP 1: K Takes Her Coffee at the Beach
(From "Ode to Meaning")

Ocean becomes Russian or Osiris or just a gentle hush
Its blue becomes new or breezy or liquid or bright

As day breaks for K and her brilliant life,
The sun, a lemon smudge against a greasy sky,
K sits, coffee cup hot on a knee, and looks out
The sea, a shimmering plate, as thin and fragile as foil,
Seems to her a map of a future that she's fine with

I know I've spent too much time here
Up at the rail, looking at her watching the beach
Knowing I should be there with her but also
That I won't, for I am too far away to feel the waves
Or see, with any clarity, how the sea grass moves
I need to break or at least explain away this distance

**RP 2: Rufino Tamayo's Nude
(From "Impossible to Tell")**

Rose petal pink and lilac blue
Between a purple staircase and
An explosion of yellow stars
She sits erect, looking away
His nudes are like that – bodies you understand
Holding up heads that are like slices of fruit
Like a poem by Robert Frost that takes you
Where you expect to go but then veers away

I saw her first thirty years ago in a gallery out West
Owned by a small man in a patched pullover
I wanted her, but he told me to be patient
To look a hundred times before deciding

But I was impatient and couldn't wait
Because everything looked so damn promising then
Not just Tamayo's nudes but the lonesome drinker
The unclimbed mountain and the unread book

So she is mine and I don't regret it yet
I've learned to look a hundred times and
Especially for the part that's missing
Or doesn't fit neatly or seems false in any way

In Her Eyes and in Her Voice

In her eyes I see winter's hope
The downhill racer's powdered spray
White shouldered mountains
Spider veins in thin ice
In her voice I hear ice cracking
Coltrane coughing on the porch
Dylan sneezing in winter wind
Amadeus, pale and thin, shivering

The Muse's Body

Your mouth is a crater
From which fire and all
Kinds of burning debris
Is expelled

Your heart has a molten core
Hot with eager unreason
Fed by the brushwood
Of certainty

Your mind is the immaterial sky
A space that contains nothing
But whatever passes
Through it

The Places in Her Head

These are certain precincts in her mind
Strange neighborhoods at whose borders
I have stood immobile, fearful, watching
Hooded creatures walk down gloomy streets
Watched by whores in darkened doorways
Beneath a darkening sky
But there are parks there and gardens too
Havens green and flush with life
And limpid brooks whose grassy banks
Afford the wary traveler a safe respite
And in between there are vacant lots
Of broken parts and shattered bits
That once were new and gleaming
And could, I think, be so again

Not an Argument, Exactly

Not a riposte but a fleeting
Movement of the eye
That tells you he does not
Believe you – not now or ever more

Not a complaint but a limpness
That supports nothing
Not even the slender hope
Of standing later on

Not an answer but a gesture
That raises a question
You don't want answered
But feel you need to know

Not an apology but a shift
Of posture that begins
A second conversation
One you've had before

Not an argument but a shadow
At the periphery of your mind
The sun blocked momentarily
By the moon passing by

A Question of Feeling

I asked you if we would choose each other
If, had we not had this long life together,
These nearly forty years of intermingling
And had all the things we made out of it
Our boys, this house, that bin of photos
The stuff we acquired along the way
Separately or together but mostly separately
And all the inadvertent causes and effects
You said – the question needn't be asked
And still I asked it and you answered
You said that I would not choose you
And hearing that, I said the same
We were quiet after that and in that quiet
I knew how well and deeply I was lying

What Poetry Is Not
(For Édouard Glissant)

Not a fuck you to history
Written by timorous men
Ass kissing their conquerors
With jimmy-rigged mythologies

Not an antipode to war
Initiated by greedy cunts
Breaking through a thin shell
Of civility for profit or pride

Not a refutation of plundering
Or the razing of living forests
Or the spewing of deadly toxins
And all that other stuff

But something untethered
To what we want to believe
More like startled birds ascending
Just beside your line of sight

Crooked Stick

My love is a crooked stick
But it's all I have to support me
In passion's quicksand garden

I make love by thrusts and flailing
Cutting limbs, spilling the fruit
Making a messy path forward

The ground now is thick and heavy
And can't support my greater weight
I'm sinking and yet still holding this broken stick

At the Café alla Umbria

What's with the waitress?
Her, in the black dress
She has a killer body
And beautiful eyes
But she looks unhappy
Not existentially
But like she's not pleased
To be here
And taking it out on us
When bad behavior is dressed
In youthful beauty it's something
Other than bad, it's interesting
And excusable – no, worse
It's fetching – why is that?
It's because you believe
You have a secret power
That you lack

Everything, Then Dust

Walking along the boardwalk this morning
I felt like everything was just as it should be
And yet I could not stop thinking of you
When you couldn't speak any more
And your mouth was a thin line that said no
And your eyes were tunnels to my fear of death
You were a living corpse on its way to powder
And this morning, so many years later, I knew
That even back then I was that body too

The Party

At our artsy party on the poolside veranda, they
assembled
All the great ones, talking about the old days and the
great dead ones
When one of them, somehow tired of years and
years of parties
Who had been not only one of the great ones but
also a champion
A champion of something, maybe throwing the discus,
And held the record for more than forty years
(This, I didn't know, I admitted – I was, in fact,
impressed)
And had a certain flair
And his size, his physical presence,
Was an added bonus – a huge man with a white
ponytail and a scar
That ran down the side and then around his neck
(He didn't say)
Went into his bag and took out a long handsaw and
a bow
And began to play like there was something playing
through him
And the music built up to a terrible crescendo and
we shouted
You are the Greatest of the Great Ones – and he
smiled and shook his head

In the Cage
(After Timothy Donnelly's "Malamute")

I spent several hours every day standing there
My hands, knuckles white, gripping the cold steel bars
Looking up at the small window high on the
opposite wall
That looked down onto the parking lot below where
My R's 1962 Pontiac was parked, the dope still hidden
In three little hide-a-key cases under the dashboard
And remembering our short but "momentous" trip
And how he left me when his father bailed him out
And when the trustee came in, his chains clinking,
I looked at him at first with curiosity and disdain
For I could see that he was in one way, and at one time,
Like me – but that he had evolved into something else
Something I didn't envy or admire but vaguely feared
And I was shamed when, seeing me, he smiled meanly
As if he too saw a common connection but he was
or felt
Way, way beyond that now, and he was proud and
pitied me
And everyone like me
Yet I could also see that our proximity made him
afraid of me
Not fully but in some small part of his brain
That I had some amount of strength he lacked
And could, as he passed by, reach out and grab his neck
And pull his lesser body towards me and against the
steel
And hold his head against the bars and bite off the
tender

93

Parts of his face
And thus I stood up and moved toward him
And he backed away and that made me laugh
And that happened the next day too
But the thing is, on the third day
I looked away from him
And he no longer smiled at me

If I Have to Wait

If I have to wait that long for you, you'd better bring
    me back something
A good book, a braided leather wristband, a box of
    Belgian chocolates
Or your bare white thighs under a short plaid skirt
You've got your own sense of what is fair
But remember, you started this, not me
And don't kid yourself about reincarnation – it's not
    happening
We have to make do with what we have now
So figure what my time is worth to you and then
    multiply that
By the time you will keep me waiting… and pay up

Again With More Color

The early years were lilac
The color of Easter egg shells

Then there were the yellow years
Our two years in Africa
Years of mud and dust and sky
When we lived like pioneers

Later, the good and easy green years
The natural world was so full of it
Not just trees and grass and ferns
But also my Irish eyes

These are the red years
Traffic lights, stop signs, brick walls, blood
At night sometimes I wake hurting
And I am alert to what is coming

What is coming of course are the white years
My hair, my beard, my skin
All the unpainted wood
And my mind

What Were We Thinking?

Wrapped tight around a firecracker
We rocketed to the moon
There was nothing that we feared
Except getting caught and stopped
Half naked in the winter on the bridge
We jumped into the icy river
Or, when no trains were in sight,
Touched the third rail
Or drove drunk through the dark streets
Or snuck into graveyards to dig for relics
And more and more…
Fledgling birds lifting into the night
What were we thinking?

My Library

Arise, Whitman says, the day is just before you
To work, Rand urges, seize morning's advantage
Downstairs in the kitchen Mortimer Adler waits
To tell me over eggs and bacon that most of what I
believe is not true
From the piano room the Americans (Hemingway,
Faulkner and Twain)
Command me to remember who I am even if I am not
While from the staircase Pound shouts to make it new
I don't remember inviting them or how they arrived
But I don't have the courage to send them packing
And so I am pushed through the day, a lost boy,
Lost in the Peter Pan world of my imagination

Friendly Conversations

P and I talk about real estate, about tenants and
collecting rents, about leaking roofs and bad
plumbing and air conditioners that grow old too
quickly and must be replaced and about how
hard it is to rent some units. And when we talk he
seems unhappy. But when we talk about golf, and
we always eventually talk about golf, his mood
improves. Unfortunately, there are only fourteen
conversations one can have about golf. P's gift is that
he is equally happy with them all. So we talk first
about real estate and then about golf and then we
slip into a comfortable silence, which reminds us of
how long and strong our friendship is.

J and I talk about exercise, how I'm a "pussy"
and not willing to work out as hard as he does
and how his other clients are complaining all the
time and how they get on his nerves and how he
sometimes can't find time for his own exercise. If
the conversation turns to golf, as it sometimes does,
we start to have one of the fourteen conversations
but stop ourselves and agree that we hate golf.
What we don't talk about is everything else, which
is practically everything, the huge obliterating
loneliness that we both know he feels as much as or
more than I.

A and I talk about people, how K is so relentless
in her requirements, how B does so much without
asking for help, how P is happiest when he's talking

about golf. And then we talk about us, about how we are together, as friends, how we've changed or haven't changed since we were kids. And then sometimes we talk about movies and books and life. There is always something more that needs to be said, but we do not say it. When that gap appears he fills it with his humor, his unfailing humor, and I know that means he is worried that something could be lost. In between the humor I slip in what can fit, thin little slices of my biggest, softest notions, knowing that everything is heard and will best be heard like that.

Those Phone Calls

I am always busy when you call
You always call to ask a question
A question that is never a question
A challenge or an interrogation
Accused I want to flee the jurisdiction
Drive a getaway car across the border
Or sneak aboard a flight to Spain
Even as you are speaking I am leaving
Putting on sunglasses, growing a beard
Booking a room at the hotel in Madrid
I am already drinking rum in the evening
Knowing I won't be recognized
But then you ask me a real question
"Am I listening?" you want to know
And I want to be but I'm not

General Lee

Later, amid the smoke and canon fire and slaughter
He could watch his girls gathering irises
In a meadow behind him and reminisce
About the old days, about his mother
Who taught him good manners and
His father who loved freedom
And was beaten badly for it
That was the last he saw of him
And so he became a man while still a boy
A great solder, Washington's equal,
Roosevelt said. The greatest of all
Modern warriors, Churchill believed.
He who feared foreign entanglements
Who fought for slavery and yet
Never owned a single slave
Who could have led a Yankee army
But would not turn against his state for,
Like his father, he loved freedom, or
Maybe not freedom exactly but the
Idea that he would not himself be ruled

The Snapping Turtle

He stood, in the summer's heat, on the bank
His uncle in front of him, knee-deep in the dark water
Holding one end of a limb that was being pulled away
In abrupt little tugs by something in the water
Tug by tug, it resisted stubbornly but finally
It was drawn out and he could see it and it was big
A big old, grass-stained snapping turtle, squatting
In the muddy bank, its jaws still locked on the limb's
end
Then the old man released his grip and yet it stayed
there
And he watched it and it seemed to be breathing heavily
While his uncle went up to the cabin to fetch his gun

Utter Bullshit

Next to an outsized painting of a blue ball
On a field of shimmering orange
The title card reads:

Marxism Ascending

At the base of a bronze sculpture
Resembling a blood-engorged phallus:

Hegelian Dialogue Number Four

Before entering the main exhibit hall, you see this
placard in Helvetica type:

*Demonstrates the tension between
the aesthetics of intellectual diversity
and the pathos of feminist culture
in the major media today.*

Inside, a series of ragged tee shirts
Hang, beside them, in pencil
Numbers in random order

For Amy Lowell

All night our conch house was outer-walled with rain.
Drops fell, detonating on the tin roof,
Ping! Kaplow! Pellets flattening into disks
That ran over the copper gutter in sheets of whoosh
And splashed and spattered on the concrete below
For hours the storm howled and thundered,
And the slats of the shutters shuddered
And the words you were shouting into the fury
Sprang up and flamed – orange torches in the dark!

For Emily H

There are these flowers
with centers like liquid

hollows up close
whose sharp edges

melt like a liquid trick.
An illusion is usually

dark at the end.
An illusion is a thin

curving for some
straight intent

a colored line
tracing the invisible

a straight vein
to the false heart of the plot

For Gabrielle C

You told me this: the carpet was useful
Reducing the chances you'd slip into
A fast-forward tumbled life without
Breaking places to stop and see

That there was something about it
Like the friction of a child's mind
That gives a view of what I see now
The image of my own self – racing

You told how the late summer sun
Oppressed you and made you flinch
And yet you still remember that
The treads were covered in burgundy

I like how you talked about the trees
And the sky and the blackbirds
It was enough to make me wish
Like Richard Cory, I was in your place

I remember too my own childhood staircase
And how every climb up or step down
Foretold something, became something
Not just the fastest way home or out again

Hard Stone

I've studied as many tombstones as textbooks
Looking for reassuring old stories and new clues
That would give me hope of some continuity
I've found some in bluntly or finely carved
Objects of art, cut into the hardest stone
But finally what I see
Are the signs of erosion –
The surface oxidation, the pitting and fading –
Even in the best marble that money can buy

Along the Beach

Grief in the wet sand
Where the boundless ocean
Meets the welcoming land
Where once she walked
Early morning's edgy hope
The sun a thin rim of fire

Grief in the silver buttonwoods
Their leaves wax paper maps
Tracing her hikes, first to me
And then away, into the afternoon's
Too bright blanket of choice
The sun a plate of steel

Grief in the sea daisies
Covering the space between
The searing sand and the cool sidewalk
Where her thoughts were fire and ice
Her steps hot blood on a cold floor
The sun a wheel of stone

Frank Lloyd Wright

Innovation grows from courage
That buds from a seed of pride
Rooted snugly in a mixed soil
Of ignorance and arrogance
The ignorance to imagine
A lifting away from earth
The arrogance to believe
In flight and in living
Higher than we should
Or might or will or can
And audacity too
To imagine that which
With luck we will later call
Innovation
This is what the critics forget
For there is nothing
Less courageous than criticism

Crazy Beautiful

In Barcelona time and space are relatively
Approximate to time and space back home
But with a slight tilt, one moment this way
The next moment that way and what
You think you know about form and function
All those solid ideas built brick by brick
From the books you read on art and architecture
Begin to change shape, to melt into liquid forms
"We have graduated a madman or a genius,"
Gaudi's master said. "Only the future will tell."
And the future, you know as you are walking
Down the tree lined boulevards, has arrived
And it is speaking a kind of poetry to you

The Percentages of Truth

When I said 90 percent of life is pain
I didn't mean it
Nor when I said we are 80 percent alone
Last night I said that when I turn 70
I will stop working and eat only pasta and drink
only wine
And even that, an idea I want to believe,
I didn't truly mean

I've been saying things I don't mean
For as long as I've been speaking
Sometimes I wonder why – it's like
To avoid moving toward the mean
I feel I have to be mean-spirited

I used to think you worried
You would lose me
And that fed the little boy
With a hole in his stomach
That will always be hungry

But now I know it's not worry
But a sort of recognition
That there is a tissue
However thin
That connects what we say
Not to who we want to be
But to who we are

We Settled on Three

Who is that child in the distance
With your bright eyes and my dark hair?
She is always at the edge of my vision
Elusive, ephemeral, moving away
Clutched, in her fist, a dry seed
That was to be her, our fourth

The White Room

Come in, sit down, relax
You are in the white room
Don't resist the feeling
You are having right now
It feels like force only because
You resist it –
There is no force in the white room
Close your eyes or leave them open
It makes no difference
This lightness, this lack of weight
You are feeling – it is nothing
It is what you knew would happen
In those moments when you knew
This time would come –
That time of no time
This time of nothing but
Light, white space –
Relax. Enjoy.
Everything is easier
In the white room
Everything –
Stretch out your hand
Feel the edge of the universe
Look up, see the ocean bottom
Look down, see the glittering stars
You are in Warsaw or Bruges
Barcelona or Amsterdam
Anything can be what it is
Or what you want it to be
In the white room –

A swan inside a soap bubble
A green apple on a bed of fire
A flock of cats ascending
Release yourself –
Yes, it feels strange now
But remember
It's relative and this is new
You have known gravity
But this is its opposite
The lightness of the white room
Inside you, emerging…

Early March

It is good to wake up now, empty
Cleaned out, ready for the spring
Having nothing in me,
I'm a child again, tearing open
The wrapping paper of a gift
I unwrapped yesterday and
Will unwrap again tomorrow

Here's to Uncle Tom

Here we were again, the family
The big table, the wine and food
Talking about Liam's wedding
There was so much to talk about
Helen's search for new shoes
Joanna's plan to lose two pounds
Rick's reluctance to go at all
Someone raised a glass to love
And looking up I noticed
At the top of the bookshelf
His ashes in a rose-glass urn
We had placed there the year before
Having no better idea of where to put it
And so, by forgetting, he was included

The Box, After 30 Years

During that last spring she wrote eight letters
A gargantuan task considering her
Fingers, once agile, now curled inwards
Her illness an unnecessary rebuke to an
Accomplished and still promising life
One letter for each of her eight children
Eight gifts she wanted to give them when
Her body had nothing more to give
Yet in writing them she understood
That what you want to give
Cannot be given in a letter
That what you want to say –
Embrace life, be loving, seize the day –
Can be said but never understood
Till it is, as it was, too late…
And that all you can really give then
Is your regret…
I keep mine in a tin box beside my bed

Driving Home With Uncle Lou

Lou says he doesn't like strip clubs
Though he's been to a few
He'd rather sit at the bar,
His back to the stage
Talk to the lady bartender
In a bra and lace underwear
 "The whole pole dancing thing –
There's no mystery in that,"
He tells us, exiting the highway
We are in the back seat, holding hands
It's late in the afternoon after a rain
The windows are foggy,
The landscape blurs
I can hear what you're thinking
And wish I could shut him up
But I can't and so he goes on
It will be an hour of driving
Dangerously for there is always
A chance that some shard of the past
However small could pierce the
Thin skin of our memory and
Deflate the buoyancy of this
Journey

To Beatrice
(From Baudelaire Through Robert Lowell)

It was last year at this time and in this place
That I first thought to give this race of lovers
A contest that would put us apart – that is to
Wound your pride, damage my heart, and
Stir up winged demons of the dead to alight
Like vultures in my head or rise up and
Scout with sharp eyes small movements that might
Signal weakness in you or, swooping down,
Gobble up the preacher and the clown or,
Ripping flesh from bone, shout blasphemies

But sit now – let's watch this all at leisure and
Count the missing beats and measure the
Full length of our lives, tell the mountebank
To prod forward the next upon the plank
For every man must play his scripted role
Win some battles but then at last lose his soul
While in the gardens swarm the fecund bees
Increasing love with sweet indecencies and
Giving the poet an informal education in
Nature and to death its declamation
That all we know of life begins on high
And ends with putrid corpses and the cry
Of carrion birds that sail upon the backs
Of lions and jackals that hunt in packs
Replacing what is living with the dead

Rise Up, Baudelaire

Tell me that your heart doesn't start again
When in the dark ocean of your long death
You sense a new tide rocking you gently
Lifting your body up from its sandy bed

Rise up toward the sunlit surface
Let the saltwater run through you
And clean out your sins and shame
Float gently then on the living sea

Let the current take you to the beachhead
And leave you lying on the shore
With the morning sun to warm you
And a gentle breeze to fill your lungs

Snake on a Rock

Still dark, in sandals I hiked down the old road
that runs along the stream and through a small
hammock of cypress, coconut palms, and seagrapes
to the estuary, where I found a flat rock on which to
sit and watch the morning open up.
From a crevice in the seawall beside me a black snake
slithered out and passed just beside my bare feet and
then slipped almost noiselessly into the water.
I sat there for a long while, looking down into the
sparkling black and then lay back and closed my
eyes and let the sun warm my chest and legs.
In the distance I heard the waves breaking and now
and then seagulls squawking on the shore and I also
heard the water lapping and then I dreamed...
I dreamed of everything – everything I had ever
done in my life and in our life and everything in
between and then I dreamed of nothing.
When I awoke it was lying next to me, almost as
long as I am, basking in the sun,
And it startled me, but then I could see that it was
dreaming too and so I lay back and closed my eyes
again and rested, feeling good about everything I
had dreamed and everything I had done and softly I
fell asleep again but this time I did not dream.
Later, some time later, I woke up and the sun was
behind a cloud and it was gone.

At the Center

Just a mile before Jacksonville
As you roll up A1A beside the ocean
Just after a stretch of Australian pine
You'll see a place on your left, by itself,
Marked with a sandwich board: "Bar and Grill"
A wooden shack with a plywood porch
In a sandy lot under coconut palms
Walk directly to the very back and you'll see him
At a table beside the jukebox, sitting alone
He will be just about what you expect
Bearded in a Panama hat with sunglasses
He will be drinking tequila, but the old kind
And smoking "only" Cuban cigars
Sit down and introduce yourself
Tell him you'd like to buy him a drink
And after a few he might be willing
To answer all your questions
Including the ones you are most afraid of
For he is, as he claims, the center
And you and your past and future
Have been circling around him all your life

Starless Night

No stars for us tonight
But we've these thin clouds,
Whispers of distant thoughts
And in the morning, perhaps
A soft drizzle… a warm jacket of fine rain

What can we do without that extra
Brightness to blind out our fears?
Or get from these silken ambiguities
Vague white whisked thoughts or feelings
Receding into the dark?

In the corner of the room
There is a shadow that alarms me
It is a memory or even a kind of prescience
That something – then or now or later,
After a night storm perhaps –
Will assert itself and we,
Tired of struggling, will just quit
And that will be "okay"

And so we must ignore these fears
And try to make every bit of what has passed,
Remembered or not, into vapor or mist –
Anything warm, ineffable and beautiful – and
Sleep and wake into a better place
Because, if not, then what?

Everything Shimmers

Everything – even the air – shimmers still
When, back from town, I am sitting here
Comfortably on the porch, looking at the lake
Listening to the crickets and now a thrashing –
Some small animal moving in the scrub trees
I am sentimental like this when, against all odds,
I can get back here an hour before sunset
When there is still some light on the grass,
On the rowboat, on the front of the cottage
Remembering how when we were young
We came here with a sharp sense of joy
That brightened the edges of everything
Including imagined things such as nearly all
Our plans and expectations of the future

Silly Little Waterfall

It's the size of a washbasin
Three limestone rocks
One hyacinth, some ferns
A shallow pond, a tube, a pump
And clear running water
It's so artificial it's almost comical
And nothing lives in it, nothing could
Yet beside it I can sit and work
The water's trickling a comfort
To the sometimes unsettled atmosphere
Of my mind that, however hopeful,
Can be so easily dampened by trouble
Or chilled by recalcitrant memories
Or moved like meadow grass
First gently and then suddenly put down
Flat as a storm passes overhead

What It Is You Have

Where are you now?
At home, struggling
I know – it matters
But I won't call

Here is what I could say:
That you should come here
Deliver your troubles to me
And I will sort them out

But we have tried this
Seven times seven hundred times
And it has not worked – never
And those failures make it worse

So if I call you, the only thing I could say is this:
I have a sense of your sensitivity
You have the reins of my attention
Not what you're looking for, but a lot

Self Improvement

Step One:
Count up the wrinkles on your hand
Subtract the lovers you've forgotten
Add the kindnesses you've given
Divide by the Saturdays you have left
That's your number

Step Two:
Take a taxi to a tattoo parlor
The nearest one is fine
Pick a font – a bold one in black
Then select a finger – any one will do
Have the number inked along the inside

Step Three:
Go back to where you came from
Your house or some house in your mind
On the kitchen table put a cutting board
Select a knife – the sharpest is the best
Cut off the numbered finger and start again

A Writer Gets Old and Sick and Dies

At 30, when I met him, he was already old
Briefly sober, his hand shook when he lit cigarettes
We were friends and fellow workers for 30 years
But did not talk in earnest until he got sick and then
The stories came and came and came and I knew
Why he could forgive every sort of weakness in me
But nothing – not even at the end – in himself

Mambacho in the Clouds

Eternities ago, when the earth was vapor, an Indian
spirit or god or other thing lifted its feathered head
and belched fire that enflamed the sky and shook the
earth, which cracked and opened up and vomited
these many rushing rivers, cutting channels through
the lava-black terra and filling them with *aqua pura*
while fissures below shifted, moving mass in one
direction and the other while vast planes dropped
and mountains rose and hollows filled with liquid
and moss and green covered everything –
Oh, Nicaragua, how young you were!

Meditation in a Pagoda by the Pond

Even the pond's surface troubles me
The way the scum collects at one end
Although the sun's reflection on the surface
And the reflection of the pagoda and the
Breeze – happily a breeze – is nearly
Just as it should be… still
I can't help but remember a trip
Some trip, there were many like this
When I was busy with my work and
You were off with your fellows far afield
Busy with interruptions as journeys are
(How many times I tried to tell you that
When coming back from China or Japan
I found you there but already half gone)
And so I learned how sleep's vacancy
Can be filled up with vanquished fears
And when you surprised me at my work
Home a day too soon (or was I wrong?)
I could not tell what was left of us
Nor can I know precisely
Everything I missed while you were gone
It is enough to sit here in the shadows
And watch the rippled mirror of the sky
Knowing that beneath the water move
The pretty, muscled koi fish that cannot
Breathe if they do not move and yet
Grow and find a size for life that equals
Whatever circumscription is allowed

Act III, Scenes 1-6

Brown whiskey, dirty glass, corner table
The jukebox playing *En Questa Tomba Oscura*

Outside in the alley, a shaft of pink light
Blinks on the brick face of a factory wall

She walks in, an ostrich, preening,
Click-click on the hardwood floor
Candles in dishes along the back bar flicker

Man at the table in the corner, listening
When the music stops, his breathing stops

We measure the long distance
Between him and the microscopic reflection
Of his body in her blue eyes

He stands finally and looks up
She hesitates, just briefly, and walks by
He sits. Sips his whiskey. The music resumes.

Inevitable

Along life's route a sign is posted
"Everything disintegrates persistently"
The closer you come to the end, the bigger it is

My father was angry
He had still, at 81, lots of things to do
Books to write, places to see, promises to keep

Kieran felt cheated
He'd wasted so many years, drunk
He believed he should get those years back

Melissa was relieved
Or so she said
And yet
She spent that last year writing letters

Up on the Roof, 1969

Hot on the top of the flat back roof of a factory
The tar shimmering in the summer's brutal heat
We worked in the same tar-splattered tee shirts
And tar-splattered jeans and tar-splattered boots
But the men, who were black men,
Held their hair down with kerchiefs
While we, the young white boys, wore caps
Charlie, our foreman, lay down the hot stuff
Swabbing the deck, his forearms thick as tree trunks
And black and gleaming and dropping sweat that
Crackled when it hit the dry felt tar paper,
He sang, "I got a girl named Tony Moroni"
And we all – the black men and the white boys –
We all did the "da-da-da-da-da-dah-da-da-da"
That kind of work worked better with a song
And seemed for that bit of time made us as one
So we did not have to think that in September
We boys would return to college while
Charlie and the other men stayed on,
Working through the fall and winter and spring
When they would sing other songs
Songs that we would never learn to sing

On Another Roof With Peter

We were house painters, Peter and I
And lovesick with latex paint
Benjamin Moore's Semi-Gloss
It clung to nylon bristles like cream
Coated dry shingles like melted butter
We devised a mythology about ladders
Ascending instruments – god-given
Entrusted to us for our adventures
We moved up and down them like viceroys
Bringing coded messages to the roof spirits
Transforming the landscape as we worked
The best houses were the dark or dreary ones
That we bloomed, like gods, into brightness
We loved too the tall houses whose eaves
Were higher than even the ladders could reach
Extended to the realm of maximum danger
Then we would abandon the ladders
And shinny up the drainpipes to the top
And then, up on the floor of heaven, get stoned,
While *Up on the Roof*, the actual song,
Played over and over again, we sang
And moved out to the edge at the gutter
One holding the other's legs as he hung
Hip at the limit, torso folded over the edge
Forty feet above the concrete patio
And flew in the freedom of our trust

The Effect of a Good Thought

I was done walking the dream
Done with the tiger on the lamp posts
Done with the slatted sunlight on the floor
Done with hope, done with inspiration
And yet this morning you said something
I can't even remember what it was
But it made me change my mind

Still Life

Still. It was still, but still breathing
When I found it lying on the lawn
Feathers wet, wings broken, eyes alert
I wondered how long it had been there
For already the maggots were on it
Like churchgoers at a summer picnic
The sun was hot. I was barefoot and
Twelve years old with only
The meager resources of a child
I had rescued other creatures but
This one, I knew, I couldn't save
So I put weight on its skull and pushed
First gently and then with more force
And it broke softly like a hard boiled egg
I thought to bury it but didn't
The next morning it was nearly gone
Except for bits and pieces of bone
That were being picked clean by ants
I stood there, amazed, feeling half forgiven

Catechism Dreams

I was back in church again, standing at my mother's
side, astonished by her singing
Which seemed to me, having been so long with the
nuns, the definition of divine
But I was also troubled by the colored carvings of
the Stations of the Cross
That were posted on the fluted columns that ran up
and down the nave
On Thursday afternoons, after classes, Father Brown
would tell us
Wondrous stories of saints and sinners and about
the one and only truth
For which legions of faithful suffered and/or were
martyred and in doing so
Were escorted into some enchanted ever-after life of
gilded clouds and angels
And divine light and celestial music and other
wonders we could not imagine
In private he warned us each about all the mortal
sins we might commit but
Especially, since we were "that age," the sin of
masturbation, for which we'd be
Damned forever if we didn't reduce our sinfulness to
a reasonable degree

To EH, in my Sixty-Second Year

Sixty-two: I summon the sixty-two that was in you
Back when, in Michigan, facing the long winter,
And after so much determined, robust living
You took a measure of your life

I summon the images that yet remain
The pale blue sailboat, the bleached white sand,
The red blood on a toreador's decorated sleeve
These images won't be leaving soon

I have my own memories – equal to yours
And at sixty-two I too feel somehow cheated
I get it and yet I can't help but wish that you hadn't
And wonder whether I might do the same

Cleopatra

This is our favorite bathroom. You can see how we
styled it. The Asian tapestries. The Chinese Buddha
resting on his side. Look at this *kalik* – the fine silver
threads, attention to detail. That aroma? Incense and
cologne.

We are alone at last, you whisper

We debated macroeconomic theory. Your ideas, I
said, were for the young and the beautiful or drunken
old rich. I showed you my math: what freedom costs
and what it yields. You said I was cynical. I asked why
smart girls marry wealthy men. We covered all that.

We are alone at last, you whisper

We had traipsed from one place to another just
to please you. We had drunk whiskey and wine
and cognac too. We had eaten figs and cheese and
tomatoes, all to please your palate. But you were not
satisfied. You were impatient still.

We are alone at last, you whisper

You are disappointed with all your past lovers.
You'd "given them" years of your amazing beauty
and were not happy with the returns. Having given
you everything they had, they were astonished at
your sorrow. They crumpled or charged. It didn't
matter what they did. Like me, you could never have
enough.

Fireflies and Lizards

After the sun set the fireflies came,
Lighting up the yard, points of hope,
Surprising us again and again
The air, already warm, became sultry
We sat there, too lazy/happy to move
In the tall grass beside us a lizard
Opened its mouth, its tongue searching
Like us for something we felt we
Were meant to have, but knowing that
Even those that sit still and watch
Must work to eat, sleep to dream
And wake again hoping for something
Both good and unexpected, then
Sleep and dream and wake again

We Would If We Could

Pascal is back in New York City
After a successful exhibit in Paris
But cannot have lunch with us today
I'm in the hospital again, she texts

We wonder what we should do
But don't know what she needs
Some kindness surely – not much
A quick visit or a phone call

Lacking definition, we have maxims
Life is short, seize the day
We cannot carry Pascal's burden
So we stay in touch

Morning Shower

In the shower, shaving, I cut the skin beneath my
chin but didn't stanch the bleeding
I stood there, under the hot water, letting it bleed
until… well, until I would bleed out
That was the plan, but it didn't happen
It just kept bleeding and the shower water made
Pretty pink rivulets that found their way down my
chest and thighs and feet
It was a lovely long little moment until something
changed
And I dried myself and said fuck it and went about
my day

Rulers of the Earth

We find them
Revolting
But to be fair
They were here
Four hundred million years
Before we arrived
We are, thus, their guests
And the world we claim as ours
Is really their world
We, not they, are intruding
We, the large, unsightly
Latecomers
And in their numbers
They give us life
For every man an entourage
Two hundred million strong
Nine billion per square mile of
Habitable land – Ants alone
Number ten thousand trillion,
And weigh as much as six-point-five
Billion of us, their uninvited guests
There are two hundred ninety thousand
Species of beetles classified, millions
More remain unnamed
And we need every one of them
Every single one of them to survive

Out of the Question

I was telling you about my day because
That is what I thought you wanted
No, that's not entirely honest
Because that's what I thought we needed

I may have to take on that new business
Why?
Because I need to justify my pay
I thought you didn't need to justify anything
You know what I mean
No I don't
Why are you doing this?
Doing what?

Once again we had moved so quickly to the horizon
of our logic
Where the sea of our dark wants touches the sky of
self survival
So far away from where we were standing that the
only thing
We really ever needed was once again impossible to
grasp

Here's What I Leave You

Because you cannot ever say you need me
Because I can't admit when I am wrong
Because we are always entirely certain
That life is exactly as we see it...

I leave you this:

A ragged miscellany of misgivings
Some cardboard boxes filled with qualms
A stash of thumb-worn coins of worry
And one mint-state portrait of regret

Eighteen Words

1.
Anoesis

Give an hour a day
To unhurried thoughtlessness
And work the others

2.
Nyctophobia

Night's dark cloak on your shoulders
Memory says you will be alive tomorrow
Yet you wake gasping for life

3.
Cerulean Wishes

Three things: your unhurried love
Ambition in the morning
Stelliferous skies at night

4.
Pansophy

I've read all the books you've recommended
And still have found but what I know:
First the tightness, then the letting go

5.
Ziggurat

Oh, Mesopotamia!
You slipped away
When I was drinking

6.
Fascicle

Bundle my hopes
Bear them with you
Keep me thus

7.
Mountebank

You don't want to admit her
Yet she invades your heart
And therein makes a haven

8.
Perdition

Don't tell me about your losses
Unless you will hear mine
We are all equal in misfortune

9.
Meta-Journey

You say the road behind is empty
But I feel footsteps
Pilgrims you refuse to hear

10.
Opuscule

Thirty years' work
Is knitted here
A garment incomplete

11.
Omnibus

Everything I have
Is represented here
You require more

12.
Knavery

What you said was hurtful
But your smile was kind
In that soft net you hold me

13.
Coquetry

To possess my fealty
Laugh at my wit
Loudest at the cruelest

14.
Panegyric

There he was
A portentous figure
Then, like that, he was gone

15.
Stertor

I can't sleep when you are snoring
You can't sleep when I nudge you
We have to get some rest soon

16.
Trammel

We swim, we say, in singular paths
But when fate's unseen net is cast
We are caught together

17.
Crepitate

What's that sound, my love?
The hearth's fire crackling?
Or your hushed asides?

18.
Poltroon

I was a brave man
Then I was soundly beaten
Now I wisely hide

The Zoology of Me

Some days a seal
Heavy on land
Yet sliding
Weightlessly
Into water

Some days an ox
Hock-deep in mud
Yoked to a cart
Of its own
Bone and muscle

Some days a jackal,
Stalking prey
From a distance
And then, just then
Sprinting and striking

And some days a lion
In the shade of a banyan tree
Sitting, head up
Not idling
But waiting

Thanatopsis

From the other side and finally
She returns languid, almost spent
Her hair moist and tousled, her shoulders down
As if, having barely vanquished one battle
She is not capable of fighting another
She is almost gone and yet in her eyes
There is a ferly look that reminds you that
Her story, which you spun out in lines of silver,
Was true, but only for as long as you were spinning
And now is false and yet you cannot unearth
The idea of her from the soil of your mind
The one that, even as she recedes behind
A distant, dark sky, will reinvent her

Poetry Now

A deadly contest in an empty arena
A stumbling gait, a foolish blunder
A clean gun with a faulty trigger
A silent prayer in a church of thunder

Where love lies at the lap of fortune
Where ambition trips on the sill of care
Where truth slips from the grasp of knowing
When impulse is tethered by despair

A dizzy strobe in a darkened ballroom
A comic strip that has no name
The sum of our hopes and sorrows
Wrapped in a rubber-band ball of shame

If I Had a Hammer

If I had a hammer I'd toss it aside
And dig my hands into the earth
Push my fingers into the coolness
Excited by what I might discover
For there are more secrets below us
Than those we keep in our pockets

Or…

I'd put it on the wooden bench
In my tool shed
Then leave and close the door
And forget about it for a while
Returning, I'd be surprised
To find something so useful

Or…

I'd slip it casually into my tool belt
And let it hang against my hip
Take a walk feeling its weight
Noticing the attention I was getting
(There is nothing sexier than a hammer
In the tool belt of a handsome man)

For…

I need to decide what's more important:
To discover some transforming secret
To be surprised by what I've forgotten
Or to become a man with a gimmick

Mortal Sins

There are three mortal sins
Which all strivers must,
By design, commit.
The first is cowardice,
Which keeps them secluded.
The second is envy,
Which fuels their ambition.
The third is arrogance,
Which gives them hope.

It Could Have Been Like This

You could have been a gypsy
I could have been a fool
Our town a haunted forest
Where, lit by a campfire,
You, a flickering beauty,
Could sit, the smoke a halo
Around your golden hair
While I danced fiercely
Jingling bells on my slippers
Hoping in the ghostly darkness
To light up your vagabond heart

Hoping for a Lift

I want to be happy again
But like this candy-flavored
In-the-moment euphoria, this
Unselfconscious appetite for life

Not that medicated traipsing through
The tidy rooms of the great clean house of
Evenness where nothing bad can happen
But also nothing very good

I won't be doing the junk anymore
No, I'll press a bony shoulder of reserve
Against the heavy door of consciousness
Against whatever's on the other side

I want to be here, right here, inside this
Crisp morning with the soothing tide
But it's not easy, this happiness,
It has a big price, perhaps more than I can pay

Some Compensation

Yes, the world around you may pause a moment
While whoever is still there will huddle to say to
Whoever will listen that they knew you when or
Maybe tell a story that, now, is really a story
About nothing – for what is really happening is that
There is always an arithmetic to funerals
And they are doing the calculations
Figuring how you did this or that to bring it on
But only those things they are not doing
But soon the tide of their problems will engulf them
And they will slip back into the stream
Of the living, which, if this is any comfort,
Flows into the beautiful soulless stream of
Everything that is nothing more than you

For Someone

The boy beside me
is not you but he
is familiar in all

the important ways.
I pass through life
finding you over

and over again –
I oppress you
with love. And the

surrogates?
Afflicted by my
oppression, they leave,

leaving me to love you
again like I loved you
before I loved you.

**At His 87th Birthday Dinner
(after following the new
waitress to the register,
as reported by his son)**

His feet, size ten, were larger than hers
And her thighs were twice as thick as his –
Her buttocks, perfect half-globes of muscle,
Would have fractured his slender pelvis –
The points of her breasts threatened
The fragile hollow of his throat –
He noticed nothing but her full lips
And rosy cheeks and sparkling eyes
They were inches apart now
He saw himself as a hummingbird
Fluttering about a fragrant flower –
I saw a magnificent mantis, preying,
Unconsciously but certainly, waiting
To eat the old bird – leathery tissue
Brittle bones and all – whole

For KD Again: Eulogy in Two Voices

It was cold today – windswept and drizzly
Brittle leaves skirted across yellow grass
Even the parking lot was sad – half-filled
As if everyone only half-wanted to come

Everything was fine, and then
It went so dismally bad
We did our best to ignore it
We had so much to do

A gloomy bedlam of acolytes attended
Hopeless young writers, dreary ex-alcoholics
The remnants of your fractured life
Who knew you? Who loved you?
I couldn't tell

Let's not talk of that, not now
Let's talk about the sea stories
And that time in Osaka
When I rigged the bicycle race

With your last wife and father-in-law
I talked about nothing
I also met a nun, a distant friend,
I couldn't tell you why she was there

So what do you think of this room?
I mean really. Can you believe it?
What a fucking mess… a shithole
I'm ready, I swear, I'm ready

I thought about what I should say:
That you were selfish and beautiful?
That you were honest to abrasion?
That you died too soon?

We said we'd have no regrets
The living would have memories
And that would be enough
That's what we said

I came back to the facts:
You built your own boat
And sailed it
And wrote two good books
Inspired countless drunks
And would-be writers
And had our conversations

That last day was good – you made that joke
About Ozymandias, King of Kings
"Look at my fortunes and despair!"
And then we laughed

I studied your face and hands
The fingernails were polished
The suit – you never wore suits –
Looked good on you, oddly
You were just plastic and cold
And most insistently – gone

Connectivity

Inside the cloister is a garden
At the garden's center is a wilting rose
In its stem, a dream of blooming

A match tip becomes a flame
A flame wants kindling
Finally, a cathedral is on fire

A palm tree in the sunlight
A dancer, arms out, center stage
Suddenly a constellation forms

Gromo in Africa

From a coal-mining town in Pennsylvania he came
to N'djamena
Unshaven, unfinished and without a clue, like me
He wore a paperback book of Shelley in his shirt pocket
Played rugby and basketball ferociously (We feared him)
Walked barefoot through the dirty streets of N'djamena
And beyond, because he would not be confined to
the "safe" quarter
In those dusty hamlets he would arrive like a nomad
from the desert
Stay and move on and thus the people came to know
him
And so after a while he would be greeted at the town
limits
By school children, shouting *Gromo! Gromo est
arrivé! Gromo!*

He stayed on for a year after I left, working as a well
digger *en brousse*
There, they say, he met an ugly woman who had
been cast out and took her in
And had beautiful children with her, caramel skin
and blue eyes
Then, late one night, walking home after drinking,
he met
On the moonlit road – and this too may have been
just a rumor –
A lone white bull, standing tall, vapor rising from its
nostrils
Looking at this bullish white man on his road, it
lowered its head

But did not move and so Gromo did, he charged it
and hit that bull
In the head and the bull went down and Gromo
went down too
And later rose again but the bull did not and that is
what they say

Surprised Into Grief

While I was away last week, busy with other things,
Someone cut back the sea grass and the
buttonwoods
It was severe and it surprised me and it opened up
Inside me a space in which a kind of sorrow stays

All afternoon it rained and it was sad and pretty
I remembered how it rained in Africa, in our garden,
And how we liked to sit and look at it because it felt
Like the earth was thirsty and it was and we were too

But I wasn't sure and so too that night
When the stars came out briefly and disappeared
And returned I knew I would have seen that as
A second coming but I saw it as a fading out

How He Did It Like He Did It

Long before he shot himself he noted
There were never any suicides
Among the people one knows –
"No successful suicides, at least"

Browsing the weekend papers
He had found a few –
One "Chinese, a Norwegian and a Brit"
That had done it well and "cleanly"

But with the rest he suspected it was just
Booze and sleeping pills and dramatic gestures
Dropping off to sleep sad and simpering and wet
And waking up, pathetically renewed

Stomach pumps, soap and egg whites
Saved them on those early mornings
But later on they were all back again
In their favorite haunts talking news

He had felt his own "undoing" once
On a boat in a storm in the ocean and
Again, oddly, looking at a painting by
Sam Francis – It spurred him, he said

So really it wasn't the pain of the cancer
Or the fear of the end of whatever he had
It was more like the Chinese or the Brit
Or his prose – a job done cleanly, that's it

Fractals

In the mirror something passing
Half the likeness of a running man
It's me again, in fragments, broken
Everything now is like this –
Duplicated, duplicitous, the same

Gertrude Stein, Frankenstein

Put on the heavy metal kettle
Lay bacon down on the grill
Come and spend the day, say
It's a whole new watermelon, is it?
Take this idea, that iron pan, this dead man
Count out the beats of retreat, the slick prick
Your constant beagle, your troop of cows
Work in your nightgown, be the class clown
You are neither in the fire nor set on ice
It's so cold to be a la mode – admit it
So act nice, come to the wedding
Stand there, throw rice, redo the bedding
Where are we heading? Really?
Form follows function, function is diction
And diction is friction
Dampened out and lit up again

Climbing Mount Kilimanjaro

Ascending, your thighs and your lungs burn
Because, really, there is never enough air
But you continue because that is the idea
You think about the promises – the views
An uplifting view of descending slopes
Graceful, meandering trails down to the
Yellow plains of a mile-high desert in Kenya
Head locked in position, shoulders squared
You can see nothing but the four square feet
In front of you – your shoe tips, his scuffed heels
The gravel-covered path, the burning
This is what it turned out to be
Later they will ask you how it all was
And you will know what they want to hear
But you will say, "It was horrible, just horrible,"
Knowing that, from then on, they will think the less
of you
And you will wonder if you missed something

Confession

My sins are now so heavy fucking heavy, he says,
I swear to God I cannot bear them anymore
She remembered when he could, when he wore them
Like a thin undergarment, weightless and pliable

These days, weary at night, he goes to bed early,
And they come with him, like another body
Shaped from the contours of his outside
But rooted to his inside, holding him tight

It's like I'm inside one of those crushing machines
That's closing in but slowly, like it's timed to my
breathing
Each time I exhale and my ribcage contracts it follows
I'm losing breath and with every breath, which sucks

It is a sort of act of contrition he is making
And she, he believes, has the grace and power
To forgive him and take that weight away
We all have something we regret, she thinks,
But doesn't tell him: We all want forgiveness in the end

Next Year Maybe

Here's the plan: Move to Italy,
Rent a storefront on Via Rustica
Sell art or antiques or something
Smoke little cigars and drink espresso

Or: Fly down to Granada, Nicaragua
Get a small room at a local hotel
Write spy novels on the terrace
A Panama hat hiding my face

Or: Drive 32 hours to Montana
Camp out in the valley in a canvas tent
Read my unread books in the day
Listen to the wind or whatever at night

But here's the deal: For now, I have this room
Above my garage, beside my house,
Across the street from the ocean
Where I can, if not write, make plans

Featured Books From Cap & Bells Press
Available at www.amazon.com

Back and Out Again
By Mark Morgan Ford

This is Mark Morgan Ford's first collection of poetry. It is the end result of a nearly impossible challenge that he set for himself: to write a poem a day for a year. With a willingness to try anything, he began an exploration of the possibilities of rhyme, rhythm, and form. Inspired by his interest in everything from mythology to politics to the complexities of human relationships, he found his unique voice. In this collection, we discover a new perspective on every subject that has fueled the imaginations of poets since the time of Homer.

It Is Raining, Lovely, Raining
By Mark Morgan Ford

In his second poetry collection, Mark Morgan Ford becomes more introspective. Observing, remembering, and reflecting. Finding meaning in a moment… joy or sadness in a gesture… humor where it is least expected. With every poem, we sense a growing confidence in his own abilities.

Back From the Abyss: The Autobiography of a Low-Bottom Alky
By Kieran Doherty

In *Back From the Abyss*, Kieran Doherty takes us along on the wild ride that was his life. With a voice reminiscent of Pete Hamill's in *A Drinking Life* and a childhood as tough as Frank McCourt's in *Angela's Ashes*, he tells his story, full of wit, bravado, and Irish charm.

The Invention of Pancakes and the Parade Without the Candy:
Excerpts From the Journal of a Late-in-Life Dad
By Alec Singer

Alec was 50 years old, experienced in living, sore in the joints, recently married… and a first-time father. While his high school friends were sending their kids off to college, he was faced with changing diapers. He resolved to bear it with a grin and recorded his experiences – funny, sad, and surprising – in a journal that he shared with those high school friends. They helped and heckled him along the way, half-happy they were done with it and half-envious of the insights he had about parenting as a late-in-life dad.

A Joyous Fatalism
By Timothy Siniscalchi, with photographs by Gwen Gove

Why a book of aphorisms written by a contemporary, unknown author? Because we believe the aphorism is a valuable literary species. And without the publication of new aphorisms by new writers like Timothy Siniscalchi, the species cannot survive.

How to Speak Intelligently About Everything That Matters
By Mark Morgan Ford

This book is a compendium of nearly 2,000 nuggets of information that are essential when talking about such subjects as cultural history, literature, theater, art, architecture, and philosophy. Page by page, it will help you become a more precise and polished conversationalist. It will help you exchange ideas with knowledgeable people without feeling foolish… and with humble folk without sounding pompous. More importantly, it will give you insights that will enrich your experience of the world around you.